THE LAMB CYCLE

THE LAMB CYCLE

What the Great English Poets Would
Have Written about Mary and Her Lamb
(Had They Thought of It First)

DAVID R. EWBANK
Illustrations by Kate Feiffer

Brandeis University Press
Waltham, Massachusetts

Brandeis University Press
© 2023 text by David R. Ewbank
© 2023 illustrations by Kate Feiffer
© 2023 foreword by James Engell

Printed in China

Designed by Lisa Diercks / Endpaper Studio
Typeset in Filosofia

For permission to reproduce any of the material in this book, contact
Brandeis University Press, 415 South Street, Waltham MA 02453, or visit
brandeisuniversitypress.com

Library of Congress Cataloging-in-Publication Data
Names: Ewbank, David, author. | Feiffer, Kate, illustrator.
Title: The lamb cycle : what the great English poets would have written about
Mary and her lamb (had they thought of it first) / David R. Ewbank; illustrations
by Kate Feiffer.
Description: Waltham : Brandeis University Press, [2023] | Summary: "The rhyme
'Mary Had a Little Lamb' told in the style—and substance—of the great English poets
from Edmund Spenser to Stevie Smith" — Provided by publisher.
Identifiers: LCCN 2022036688 | ISBN 9781684581450 (cloth)
Subjects: LCSH: Mother Goose—Parodies, imitations, etc. | English literature—
Adaptations. | Lambs—Poetry. | Parodies. | LCGFT: Parodies (Literature)
Classification: LCC PS3605.W36 L36 2023 | DDC 811/.6—dc23/eng/20220829
LC record available at https://lccn.loc.gov/2022036688

10 9 8 7 6 5 4 3 2 1

CONTENTS

FOREWORD
James Engell

Absolute statements, whether in literature, science, or law, run a great risk. Yet, it seems that never have so many superb, diverse parodies of so many varied authors appeared in one collection written by a single hand. They range from Edmund Spenser to Stevie Smith, the sixteenth through the twentieth century.

Older poets and rhetoricians divided the work of composition into three elements: invention, design, and style. Different terms for these elements might be used, for example: originality, organization, and ornament. The triad indicates the concept of a work, its literary form or aesthetic shape, and its qualities of phrasing—the magic of new combinations of words.

Parody often takes a low, incongruous, or unlikely subject. All these parodies stem from one familiar invention, a nursery rhyme that children have repeated for generations, "Mary Had a Little Lamb." So, invention of story or originality of concept is not the main point here. However, to transform that little narrative into the respective designs and aesthetic forms favored by great individual writers requires deft skill. Then the unique language and idiom of each writer—word choice, phrasing, nuance— David R. Ewbank recreates with an acute ear in an extraordinary manner, reproducing the styles of the original authors, though without lifting directly from them. Ewbank even plays with the fact that none of these authors invented the story in the first place. *The Lamb Cycle* offers "what the great English poets would have written about Mary and her Lamb (had they thought of it first)."

None of this could be accomplished without intimate, loving knowledge of these poets, a love that lifts the imitations to the level of new inventions themselves. Some parodies diminish an author's work by exaggerating to excess its most recognizable features. While the titles in this volume allude to titles of poems by the honored authors, the new poems do not lampoon their models, for a lampoon aims to deflate, even destroy its object. The poems here do not satirize their originals so much as pay homage to them. The fabric of the text, the warp and woof of language, is born again, brilliantly new yet strangely familiar. These poems achieve what Samuel Johnson claimed as an essential function of poetry, to make the familiar unfamiliar and the unfamiliar familiar.

In these new creations, two levels operate simultaneously, that of the original author, and secondly that of the imitation. A surprising voltage leaps between the two and, through the shock of unexpected recognition, prompts pleasure and even laughter. The humor comes, too, from a diminutive subject harnessed to sophisticated literary forms.

Books of poetry were once commonly illustrated. Famous artists regularly turned their talents to the work of Coleridge, Milton, Shakespeare, and many American poets. William Blake and Stevie Smith illustrated their own poems. It is wonderful to see Kate Feiffer's drawings enliven with such panache the tradition of illustrated verse.

"Mary Had a Little Lamb" first appeared in print in 1830 as "Mary's Lamb," though the rhyme, associated with children's education and religious purposes, enjoyed an oral tradition, too. See, for example, *Poems for Our Children* (Boston: Marsh, Capen & Lyon, 1830); *Juvenile Lyre, or Hymns and Songs: Religious, Moral and Cheerful*, collected by Lowell Mason (Boston: Richardson, Lord and Holbrook, 1832); and *Juvenile Lessons, or the Child's First Reading Book* by J. K. Smith (J. and J. W. Prentiss: Keene, N. H., 1832). While the poem certainly originated in New England, the attribution of authorship is controversial. Somewhat different versions exist. The last four lines of the version printed in 1830 and attributed to Sarah J. Hale (lines not included in the "original" in the present book) carry this moral, spoken by the teacher of Mary's schoolroom:

And you each gentle animal
In confidence may bind,
And make them follow at your call,
If you are always *kind*.

In literature there is nothing more elusive of exact definition, yet nothing more indelible in memorable impact than the combined qualities of composition we call *style*. The word comes from *stylus*, the instrument used to incise clay tablets in the early technology of writing. A stylus makes an impression, and each individual scribe made a specific kind of impression, much as each telegraph operator develops a unique "hand" in sending Morse Code, though the dots and dashes are the same for every operator. However palpable, an accomplished literary style evades formulation. It mixes and fuses word choice, tone, rhythm, phrasing, musicality, and sentence structure—and in verse often adds features of meter, rhyme, and stanzaic form. Style can include another dimension, too, the interpenetration of substantive thought—an author's characteristic themes and concerns—with that writer's characteristic language. These poems are successive triumphs of style, echoed and amplified by imagination. Producing one would be hard enough. To produce more than thirty seems a miracle.

James Engell is Gurney Professor of English Literature and Professor of Comparative Literature, Harvard University.

The first few poems of *The Lamb Cycle* were written to amuse and
divert a class of undergraduate students who had spent a semester
under my tutelage pondering and discussing a varied selection
of English Victorian literature. On the last day of class, having
done all that I was capable of in the way of preparing them for the
impending final exam, I declared a holiday of sorts. Instead of
approaching the venerated authors we had been reading as the
formidable icons they indubitably are, why not, I thought—just for
once, no disrespect intended—kick back, relax, and poke a bit of
fun at them. Their venerable reputations being so well deserved
and firmly established, surely—or so I told myself—such trivial
levity as I was capable of provoking could do no serious damage
to their fame and glory. In this belief, I hope and believe that I
was right. My students did not object and, of course, the dead
poets I parodied could not. However, now that those original
poems and several more like them may reach an audience beyond
the classroom, my sincere wish is that a broader readership will
understand, as I believe my students did, that a parodist, a mere
impersonator, succeeds only because of the vastly more for-
midable and enduring successes of the originals he mimics. A
parodist goes beyond placing his tongue in his cheek; he employs
it in an attempt to speak *for* his model. It is, perhaps, a cheeky
presumption—or might be if the intent and effect of his imper-
sonation were to skewer and debase. That, however, was never my
intent, and my hope is that a perceptive reader will discover that
the effect of my parodies is not wily disparagement, but amused,
good-humored admiration.

In the process of creating my parodies, I learned that by set-
ting out to capture the stylistic mannerisms of a poet, I assumed

a task more consequential than I originally imagined. A conventional distinction is often drawn between matter and manner: the subject matter is what matters; the manner of its telling, its style, is secondary. Style (diction, syntax, figurative language—all of that) is a mere handmaiden to the subject matter. If she is good at her job, she serves her mistress well; if not, not. Whatever degree of truth this distinction may have with respect to prose, it does not meaningfully apply to poetry. For poetry, the manner *is* the matter. In a poem, style casts off her merely instrumental status as servant and becomes the featured focus of attention. This being so, a poem parodist soon realizes that attempting to master a poet's style and striving to empathize with his or her distinctive worldview ultimately amount to pretty much the same thing. Capturing a style, I learned, is a royal road to that happy destination to which all great literature leads—temporarily losing one's self in the enraptured contemplation of what it might be like to be someone other than one's habitual, accustomed self. An impersonator starts out meticulously imitating mannerisms and ends up understanding the man. Or woman, as the case may be. My wish is that the reading of my mimic verses will provide something of the same pleasure and self-expansion that I enjoyed in the writing of them.

 *THE LAMB CYCLE*

MARY HAD A LITTLE LAMB
Mother Goose

Mary had a little lamb;
Its fleece was white as snow,
And everywhere that Mary went
The lamb was sure to go.

It followed her to school one day;
That was against the rule.
It made the children laugh and play
To see a lamb at school.

And so the teacher turned it out,
But still it lingered near
And waited patiently about
Till Mary did appear.

Why does the lamb love Mary so?
The eager children cry;
Why Mary loves the lamb, you know,
The teacher did reply.

2

ᴖ *THE SILLY LAMBE*
Edmund Spenser

> *A sinless Damsell and her Lambe*
> *come to the Hall of Lore,*
> *And there a false, dissembling Sire*
> *meets them at the door.*

It fortunéd that on a summer day
A gentle, comely mayd that Mary hight
Across a grassy plaine did ply her way;
In garments wondrous faire was she bedight,
Yet fairer still her face, demure and bright,
That gracéd was by Beautie's ornament.
And by her side a lambe all lilly white
Did praunce and play in dalliance innocent
As nigher toward the haughtie Hall of Lore they bent.

Anon they came unto the loftie heape,
Full bravely deck'd and cunningly displaid
To catch the eyen of maydes, and eke of sheepe;
Its great facade with beaten gold o'relaid
So gaily shone it Phoebus quight dismaid
With rival light his sovereigntee to share;
The Hall was buildéd in a gladsome glade
Where flowers grew, gay blooms uncouth and rare,
That with their scent perfum'd the milde and drowsie aire.

But all without was false, fair-seeming show;
The sights within reveal'd the dolefull truth:
The fatal fruit of Knowledge bringeth woe
And eaten is in dreariment and ruth.
Inside, a troupe of students spent their youth

Persuing antient Learning's heavy tome.
All sullen-eyed they were, and old forsooth,
That whylome wanton'd carelessly at home
And freely through the fenceless fields were wont to roam.

And by the Hall's high gate a Master stood
In long blacke goune and morterboard yclad.
With gratious cheare he smiled as though he n'ould
A fly distresse, nor any wight make sad.
But though he seeméd good, his heart was bad,
And greatly he deservéd Mankynd's blame
For bringing bale to those that erst were glad.
As Sapiento was he known to fame;
In sooth Doloro was his apt and proper name.

Unwares, the guileless lambe a rule did flout,
When with the mayd inside it 'gan to tread.
The Master bar'd the way and turn'd it out,
And filled its quaking heart with fear and dread,
Which outrage Mary wexed wroth to see,
And to the cad the riote acte she read:
"Liefer had I rude remaine," quoth she,
"Than from my purest pet be severéd,"
And thence from that sad Hall her spotlesse lambe she led.

⚘ SONNET 155
William Shakespeare

That cruel hind well may the world beshrew
Who plighted pairs of sheep would separate;
Such rude divorce can but, depriving ewe,
Bank the still flickering fervor for her mate
And in his mutinous breast only beget,
By paradox, increase of fiery heat,
Stoked by inflaming hinderance and let,
Which else had burned innoxious and discrete.
How much more scorn deserves thy master's spite,
Rudely to rive from thy dark-dazzling blaze
Thy pettish fond adorer, shaggy white,
And slam the door on his enamored gaze.
Only in this, my curse, may meddling rival
Find near renown and infamous survival.

❧ TEMPER RISING
John Donne

Officious fool, what right had he
To interpose
His vexing rules and sharp, long-winded no's
Twixt Mary, sinless school-bound lass, and me?
O'erbearing pedant, he'd far better
Bar boisterous, bumptious lads from mischief,
Judge children's spelling bees by the law's letter,
Than worry wretched lambs who've woes enough
Without the meddlesome check of a dunce whose heart,
Hard as his head, would shatter Cupid's dart.

Obtrusive legalist, you mar
My innocence
To chastise me with churlish violence
And catapult me hoof o'er head down stair.
What heinous crime did I commit;
Whose tutoring would I obstruct?
Would learning cease if by my love I'd sit;
If I'm in school, can teachers not instruct?
No! Dons may catechize and scholars cram
Unhampered by the presence of a lamb.

Though severed from my maid by cruel
Infamy,
I needs must bear this short divorce from Mary,
Content that though we part our love bides whole.
The omelette egg we'll imitate;
She the yellow, I the white:

Though rule requires that we must separate,
Though I be beaten, all will soon be right;
To her gentle yoke I'll once again submit,
And thus enfolded, we'll repair the split.

❧ ACADEMIA LOST
John Milton

Of that enforced departure of the Lamb
What time it with its mistress witless strayed
Into the interdicted institute
Sing, Mother Goose, who high upon thy swift
Enpennoned mount doth scour th'empyrean
And, condescending, spur innominate bards
Of matter notable to croon: of him
Who o'er the flaming taper lept with quick
Facility; or of that jocund king,
Ancient monarch, regnant o'er a race
That fiddling men begot, who for his pipe
And bowl did lustily apply; and yet
Of her depriv'd of nose by ebon bird,
One of her greedy king's dispieséd flock.

Say, then, what moved the lamb his native haunts
To quit, forsaking fragrant pastures green
For Academe, where not the gaudy rose
Nor winsome daffodil in ample range
Delights the captive eye, but lore abstruse
In serried volumes penned delivers mind.

'Twas Mary, she who emulated not
That tender youth appareled all in blue
Whose wooly charges through the meadow roam'd
While he beneath the haystack slept; Bo Peep
Her model was, the watchful shepherdess
Who found her errant herd, though every lamb

Of tail was as devoid as those three mice
Who sightless chas'd the farmer's cruel spouse.

So lovingly did Mary mind her pet
That from the ambit of her gracious sway
The lamb was loath to go, but ever in
Her footsteps fondly followed, even through
The very door of Learning's lofty seat
Where 'mazement did its bestial wits confound.

Not meant for sheep is Wisdom's ponderous page
Which only man with profit may frequent;
Thus, when it o'er the school's broad threshold tripp'd
Did Mary's meek, adoring lamb transgress.
No willful wight may with impunity
Ignore that stern command: no pets allowed.
From out the presence of its sovereign queen
The creature was with expedition swift
Expelled. Yet even in disgraceful rout
It comfort found in expectation sweet
That to its aid, anon, the maid would come.

THE SCHOOL STEPS
George Herbert

Down this
Steep stair
He fell from bliss
And fortune fair.
Meek lamb and lettered miss,
Ill-sorted, hapless pair,
The sill of Learning's Edifice
Transgressed and made the master swear
That should he brook such sin he'd be remiss.
He pet from pupil tore like wheat from tare.
To repossess the maid and thwart his nemesis
Is now the lambkin's fervid, postlapsarian prayer.

TO MARY, TO GET OUT ON TIME
Robert Herrick

Inside the dark and horrid school
Under a miserly master's rule
Sits my Mary with her silken curls
Enbowered in ranks of budding girls—
Eulalie, Dorcas, Lulu, Pru,
Myrtle, Amaryllis—who
Can number all the golden locks,
Bright eyes, red lips, and gingham frocks
That grasping niggard hoards away
From the admiring light of day?
Come out, sweet maid, the afternoon
Shadows lengthen; all too soon
Swift thieving time robs youth's dear riches
Mauger how well the miser watches.
Come out and with a wastrel's zeal
Spend now what, later, time will steal.

ANNUS HORRIBILIS
John Dryden

All is not well in Precincts Anserine:
Misrule is loose in Mother Goose's zone!
Behold, unnatural lunar-leaping kine
And lambkins wandering lost in fields unknown.

The air's atremble with the startled shrieks
Of frightened misses driven from their curds;
No maid is safe from rhinosecting beaks,
And regal pies are strictly for the birds.

Remorseless, avicidal Sparrows kill
With minuscule but lethal bows and darts;
Aquarii, ascending, fall downhill,
And knavish thieves make off with fresh-baked tarts.

Bleak poverty prevails: a canine starves
Because its mistress cannot find a bone;
Bold larceny is rife: a robber carves
The very shift from off a sleeping crone.

A down-at-heel, shoe-dwelling termagant,
Insensible of contraception's use,
Provides her brood with meager nourishment
And then compounds neglect with child abuse.

The mighty tumble: Dumpty took a spill
That thwarted the equestrians of the town;
Like previously mentioned Jack and Jill,
Even London Bridge is falling down.

And nimble Jack, famed for dexterity,
Unluckily the candle overturned;
In the ensuing conflagration he,
Like mighty Caesar, had his britches burned.

The land is wrack'd, and yet it took this day
To compass Wreck and crown Confusion's reign;
No crime like this since Eve would not obey
And wreak'd on mankind misery and pain.

The Citadel of Learning's overthrown;
A hypocrite's usurp'd the podium.
His rants on love, ornate and overblown,
Provoke his suffering pupil's odium.

This tup-togg'd Lupus arrogates the right
That Cherubim alone may claim their own
To bar a soul, because it's fleece bedight,
From bliss and leave its mistress sad and lone.

Such shameless rape of innocence and all
The vile misdeeds that plague the realm demand
Redress; for just deliverance the call
Arises from the sore-afflicted land.

Dame Goose, retake Thy lately quitt'd throne!
Quell Anarchy! Ah, then, a grateful nation
With jubilees will claim Thee as its own
And celebrate a Glorious Restoration!

🙠 AN ESSAY ON LAMBS
Alexander Pope

Assist me, Pangloss, famed for subtle wit,
Justly to judge the plight of Mary's pet.
Disbarred from school, the lamb presumes to bleat
That God's unjust—His clemency a cheat.
Let's prove God's view is wider than our own,
And put a stopper on this sheepish moan.

1. Dumb beast, didst thou the fertile world create
Or lifeless clay with spirit animate?
Canst fathom heav'n, or plot a comet's course;
Knowst thou the universe, its end or source?
'Tis futile effort, insolent and vain,
To grasp divine intent with brutish brain.
Encompass God! One may as wisely hope
To fit the sea within a thimble's scope.

2. Fond lamb, why dost thou after knowledge yearn
And blissful ignorance so rashly spurn?
Forsake thy hopes to storm the schoolroom door;
Content thyself with humble, kiddish lore.
God wisely framed thy wits for simple tasks,
And mercifully from thee the future masks.
The knower of fate for punishment's a glutton:
Today's young carefree lamb's tomorrow's mutton.

3. Why prate about thy injuries, thou dunce!
What thou call'st evil's merely ignorance.
All bad turns good when it is judged aright;
All local pain is, elsewhere, keen delight.

The smart thou felt when teacher ousted thee
Contributes to divine economy:
No wind's so ill it bloweth good to none;
A mistress lost, for him's a pupil won.

4. Cease thy lament! How dare thou criticize!
Consider old examples and grow wise.
In Icarus view the fate of him who dares
To cast off earthly toils and put on airs;
And learn from Thebes' blind king humility:
Leave dark the future lest thou grieve to see.
Praise Eve! Although she ate the fruit and fell
And exiled us from Eden, all is well.
Sin's a mirage. In this belief be strong:
Since everything is right, there's nothing wrong!

THE VANITY OF OVINE HUBRIS
Samuel Johnson

Expelling lambs from Education's pale
Is policy no wise man will bewail.
Crowned with bay that watchful don should be
Who checks presumption, champions due degree.
Prerogatived by Nature for the sward,
Not arduous Erudition's narrow yard,
The lamb, who hates the schoolhouse autocrat
And sulks alfresco like a wayward brat,
Would rather frisk could he appreciate
That folly 'tis to aspire to man's estate.
How witless, coveting the Scholar's lot:
The patronizing Lord, the prying Scot;
The daylight lost in drudging, blear-eyed toil,
The night illumed by meager midnight oil;
Here, his labor's paid with thanks, not gold,
There, giv'n neither Praise not Pounds, he'd told
That Knowledge hath its own innate rewards,
Yet Learning payeth not thick-skulled landlords!
His days are vexed with chores he must not shirk,
With duties, fretful worry, thankless work,
Of which the worst (Philologist, be wary!)
Is authoring an English Dictionary.
Though he the prime of Wisdom's crop would cull,
Pinch and Scrape his vital spirits dull,
His youthful ardor flags, his hair turns white,
He fails and fades, Thought's harrowed anchorite.
At last, worn down by Penury and Care,
He gathers his rewards—Neglect, Despair.
His earthly goods—poor portion for his kin:

A garret bleak that lets the north wind in,
A frugal desk, some thumb-worn tomes, a globe,
Few clothes, mere rags—an oft-patched scholar's robe,
A cap, a seedy coat (a chesterfield).
His final prize? A grave in Pauper's Field.
Unhappy lamb, be silent and begone!
Getting bounced from school's a benison.

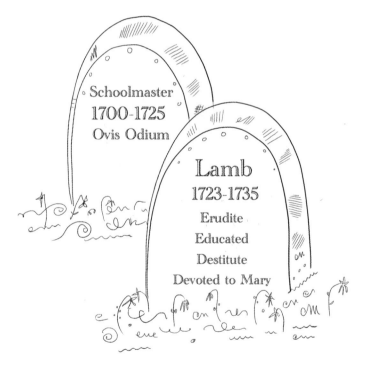

Schoolmaster
1700-1725
Ovis Odium

Lamb
1723-1735
Erudite
Educated
Destitute
Devoted to Mary

THE BOOK OF HELL
William Blake

> *Mary's Motto*
> *When the lamb, from maiden love enjoined,*
> *Becomes the bleating Beast,*
> *Then blighted is the bridal bower,*
> *Bane the wedding feast.*

The pupil of Ucant in burdened sadness paced the land,
Exiled from her fleecy mate, her gyvéd wits enchafed,
Though loud she moaned and long she looked, unanswered was
    her call,
Which echoed down Libido Vale unto the Bog of Id.
She trod upon a lowly Stone who, after crying "Ouch!",
A lecture on the private lives of pallid Specters gave.
"Everywhere mad Chaos reigns since Muthah quarreled with Dud,
Disjointed Time gives baleful birth to freakish prodigies:
The daughters of Ar in May flowers decked spurn the huddled masses
Who through the Isle of Ellis passed into America,
And beneath the banner of the Burning Bra the sisters of Era march,
And call their mates and lovers chauvinistic sons of Gunn.
Lovey, barred from Dovey, in the Boondocks wastes away,
Schizo, with Barmy and Bonkers, now resides in Loony's Bin,
Letter is from Rip divorced, and ditto Bill from Coo,
Our fathers four have had a fight—the place is like a Zoo.
Our Roomer, who's badly in arrears, roars if we raise the rent,
Beulah won't speak to Uncle Tom, and Plate One's run away with
    Spoon."
"Mercy me!" the startled maid in stark confusion shrieked,
"I'll never know Who's Who nor learn the genealogy
Of such fissiparous folk, nor ken ideal geography."
And by the Well of Enough Alone she left the chatty Stone.

EXPULSION AND RESULT
William Wordsworth

"Why, Mary, are you unemployed,
Why stand you in this lengthy queue,
And where's the lamb that so annoyed
When I last encountered you?"

Thus did I ply the dropped-out maid,
And thus she promptly answered me,
Waiting her turn to get state aid
From the Welfare Agency.

"Full four and twenty months ago
When you gave my gentle pet the gate,
I resolved to study alfresco
Beside my wooly mate.

"So dull had scholarship become
I burnt my books and scrolls and quills
And tried a new curriculum
Of clouds and daffodils.

"I delved in lore too deep for words,
A clam became my closest friend,
The dialectic of the birds
I came to comprehend.

"From trees and streams a course I took
And learned my Yews and Tees,
I acquired the tongue of the babbling brook
With which I shot the breeze.

"From Presences and Forms and Shapes
I got my higher education;
A didactic Spirit of landscapes
Taught me to take dictation.

"But my cottage in the woods caved in,
My little lamb abandoned me,
My bank account and I grew thin
In direst poverty.

"For Philosophy *au naturel*,
Though it elevates the mind and soul,
There is no paying clientele,
So I am on the dole."

∽ THE CRIME OF THE URCHIN MARY
Samuel Taylor Coleridge

Mary stoppeth
Mother Goose

It was an ancient crone who wrote
Silly rhymes for tots
Was stopped by a maid in a pinafore
With blood-red polkadots.

She cheweth her
ear off.

"To you, good dame, I must relate
A ghastly tale and garish."
"Why me, thou pale and fearsome wraith?"
"I publish must, or perish.

She encounters
two admonitory
Spirits concerning
whom Public
Statute 1743A69-4
may be consulted.

"To the schoolhouse door I skipped one morn,
My lamb, he followed me.
A grisly sprite rose up on my right,
No-Pets-Allowed was he.

"And on my left there stood a spook,
A gruesome demirep,
Her skin was daubed with somber hues,
Basic blacks and Prussian blues,
And she was Watch-Your-Step."

Mary illegally
crosseth the Line.

"Mercy, Miss, you blanch and reel,
Art thou a spirit lost?
I fear thee, maid!" "With my lamb at heel
That dreadful sill I crossed.

Her schoolmates
laugh.

"My schoolmates fixed us with their eyes,
Cold and glittering,
They clustered round, and through their
      mouths
Came ghostly tittering.

Her teacher
doesn't.

"In black, black robes the master came
The schoolroom aisle adown,
And in his hand he bore a stick,
And on his brow he wore a frown,
And out he kicked the lamb.

He exacts a
horrible penance.

"Across the board I had to write,
In penance for my sin,
'I am a naughty little girl,'
Again, again, again.

Mary curses him
in her heart.

"Ten times fifty times I wrote,
My sight grew dim and hazy.
Hour after hour, line after line,
Till I was driven crazy.

"The sun stood high above the school,
It sultry was and hot.
My toque was asoak, my guimpe was damp,
My hand did ache with writer's cramp,
My raddled nerves were shot.

"At last I heard, at end of day,
The sweetly chiming bell,
But though it spelt a welcome break,
It did not break the spell.
Still must I collar strangers stunned
My painful tale to tell.

"So long, so long, my reverend dame,
But this I'd like to say:
He writeth best who's given rest."
And quick she turned away.

The ancient crone she hobbled home—
Weary, yes, but gladded.
The tale of Mary and her lamb
She to her corpus added.

WHY DO I HATE THIS HORRID PLACE
Emily Brontë

Why do I hate this horrid place,
This dreadful, shut portal,
With recollection, glum and drear—
And fear, cold and mortal?

A dungeon's bricks and bars are clear
Of peccancy, but, ah,
Dumb, guiltless stuff can serve to wreak
Anguish! Baa, baa!

Within, a brute. His gown is black;
His sin a garish scarlet—
An ugly, faithless, evil-doing,
Cruel-hearted varlet!

And, oh, the Maid with lamb-bent eyes
And silky, shining hair,
The spring of all my wild desire,
That's left to languish there!

Banned from buoyant rambles free,
Pent in a schoolhouse smothering,
She yearns, like me, fruitlessly,
For blisses bleak and wuthering.

❧ THE REVOLT OF A LAMB
Percy Bysshe Shelley

One morn as winter turned to spring, when I
   Traversed a fragrant, amaranthine mead,
Beneath a crystal dome of radiant sky,
   From all of Custom's dull encumbrance freed
To wander blithe wherever whim would lead,
   I chanced to pass before a lowly seat
Of learning, where young scholars write and read,
   When, lo!, just like a star, but with a bleat,
A lamb shot out the door and landed at my feet.

"Apprise me, lamb," quoth I, "of your distress."
   And he this doleful story did unfold:
"My mistress is a wondrous shepherdess,
   Of peerless maidenkind the very mold;
The glory of her glance can not be told,
   Surpassing far the sunbeam's radiancy
Which stains the morning sky with orient gold
   And guilds the bosom of the surging sea
With rapturous, ethereal sublimity;

"The beauty of my Mary's lustrous orbs
   All ill dissolves into a vaporous dew
Which her benignant influence absorbs
   And doth with her sweet spirit so imbue
That everything that's fine and pure and true
   And virtuous and lofty and humane
Is manifest in splendors that endue
   The soul with blessings from the vast inane
So rare—one strives to verbalize, but e'er in vain."

"Well, anyway," said I, as from his swoon
    I calméd down the effervescent lamb,
"How chanced it that upon this fine forenoon
    You posthaste hurléd were thru yon doorjamb?"
"Within those walls there dwells a tyrant Cham,
    An ugly, evil-minded potentate;
He roams the aisles and roars, 'When I say "Scram,"
    'Tis scarce you'd better make yourself.' His hate
I earned because I sought to be my maid's classmate.

"When I beside my mistress entered school,
    The rafters rang with rude, unseemly glee
Which scored my sensitive soul with anguish cruel,
    But Mary comforted my agony
And stilled her mates with a mystic homily
    So inspirational and recondite
It was of eloquence the apogee;
    About her form there shone a nimbus bright
As though she were in Eden, clad in primal light.

"The dread despot then ordered me to go,
    But I, by Mary's courage given heart,
Rebelled—I stood my ground and answered 'No!'
    'What!' he shrieked. 'You picayune upstart!
Look on my foot, ye lowly, and depart!'
    He placed a thumping blow upon my tail
And I flew through the ether like a dart.
    Now, Poet, to the public tell my tale
That Hate may one day end on earth and Love prevail."

ODE TO COLOGNE
John Keats

Still thy perfume, Mary, tincts the air
    Like Echo's dolor dying down the dells;
Frangipanni extract, musk and rare
    Attars from Turkestan's pale asphodels
Crushed to scent-fraught essences impress
      The drowsy zephyrs of my shade-cool'd bowers
        With faint, memorial fragrance which evokes
        My absent shepherdess,
      For whose return I wait through feverish hours
        Till schoolday's end my banishment revokes.

Could mortals emulate the sweet demise
    Of scents, which linger languorous and long,
Then would I like an amorous anthem rise,
    Subsumed in vasty harmonies of song
Which ether's clement balms translate, at last,
      To mystic, measured airs which sound the sky;
        Or like a fey, frail primrose would I wane—
        Devotion's wrack'd enthusiast—
      Content that Beauty's trials beatify,
        And earn a martyr's niche in Memory's fane.

Alas, what artful anodyne can dull
    The poignant tang of Paradisal fruit?
What troche cures dis-ease? What charm, the gall?
    What Muse can lambkind's fateful doom commute?
My ardor needs must heed the interdict:

Joys by anxious absences are bought;
　　I've learned that teacher's kick and Mary's kiss
　　　　Can equally afflict.
By mistress and by master am I taught
　　To ply the pangs of melancholy bliss.

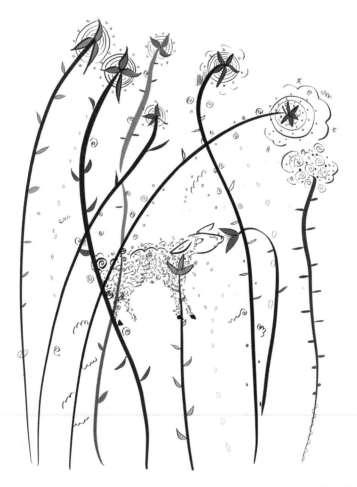

MY MAN, FRED
George Gordon, Lord Byron

Scene, a Gothic schoolroom.
Time, midnight.

Master:
The hours pass in weary, sad travail,
And each, a slow eternity, mocks rest.
Sleep, which grants my students easeful peace,
To my entreaties, wrung with keenest grief
From out the bosom wracked with pain, is deaf.
My B.A. in Black Arts will serve me now:
I'll summon forth an acquiescent sprite.

(He draws mystic symbols on the blackboard.)

Fred:
I 'aunt the regions of the Smoke
Within the sound of Bow bells,
Must 'eed the call of any bloke,
Serve commoners and nobels.

I'm 'ere to 'elp, a Cheapside shade,
On call both day and night.
All 'ours some blighter needs my aid.
Pity the poor spook's plight!

Wot's on your mind? Speak up, it's late.
You're lookin' pale and peaky.
Got somethin' on your conscience, mate—
Been up to somethin' sneaky?

Master:
Keep a civil tongue! Though wraith thou art,
I am no less! The mortal fetters which
Beclog with gross telluric clay my soul
And sorely chafe my pride I'll cast away.

(*As the Master is in the act of crushing his head with an unabridged dictionary, Fred restrains him.*)

Fred:
Now 'old on, Guv'ner! Lawks! You off your chump?
What guilty secret makes you act so daft?

Master: (*furious*)
Cease, presumptuous wraith! No creature, man
Or spirit, dares to judge. I judge my self!
My dark, all-nameless, deadly sin is mine!
No being plumbs my soul or knows my crime.
Accursed, misunderstood, I stand alone.
Enough. Obey! Call forth my loved one's ghost.

Fred:
Ghouls and goblins,
'eed this decree:
Make this bloke's love
Appear to me!

(*The phantom of Mary's lamb arises.*)

Master:
My love!

(The phantom of the lamb dies away, likewise the Master.)

An Abbot: *(who has dropped by in time to view the climax)*
Behold what God hath wrought!

Fred:
I'm blowed if this don't taik the caik!

THE CLOVER-EATER
Alfred, Lord Tennyson

The sleepy sunbeams sifting through the trees
Bespeckle all the vernal green with light,
Fragrant flowers bow beneath the breeze,
Detaining eager insects from their flight.
And in the lucent sky the birds delight;
Aloft they float, and through the ether sound
The plangent strains of pleasure at its height—
Enthralling trills that ripple and resound
Till, lo, in depths of air, they echo and are drowned.

And on the grass a winsome, wooly lamb
Grazes on the clustered clover blooms,
Pristine and new, too pure of heart for sham.
But lately severed from his mother's womb,
The lamb, all unaware of lowering doom,
Revels in careless, rapturous content—
Ignorant of guile, unversed in gloom.
And soon, his mistress, mild and innocent,
Appears, and on her pet are countless kisses spent.

Along the lane the lithe, delightful maid
Skips happily to school, and at her side
The newborn lamb, unsure, but unafraid
Struggles amain, with many a slip and slide.
Anon they come upon a meadow wide
And reach, at last, a rude and rustic school
Where Mary ope's the door and slips inside,
Abandoning her lamb. Cold and cruel
The world turns, under Grief's abrupt and tyrannous rule.

The nodding flowers cease to please; how dull
And dismal now such trivial delight
Which erstwhile made his joyous heart quite full.
Now, alone, how altered is his plight;
The daylight's luster fades and fails, the sight
Of frolicsome pleasure sickens and dismays.
But still the world rolls on, as if by right,
Despite his tears; Time brooks no delays
Nor shirks its tedious task of adding days to days.

But, hark, a sudden bell resounds, and through
The welkin rings exhilarating sound.
Sequestered in a shady bower of yew,
The lovelorn lamb leaps up and with a bound
Flies with graceless frenzy o'er the ground
To greet the resurrected Mary, quite
Immune to woe now his lost love is found.
The happy pair embrace, and still the bright
Auspicious bell peals forth the news: Delight! Delight!

FRIEDRICH SCHLAFBEWIRKEN'S EXCOGITATION
Robert Browning

Yikes! Mind your manners! That's my gown
You're treading on as if it were a rug.
It's poor reward I get, or even thanks,
For drilling facts into your rock-hard pates;
I'm thick beset with cares—spare me the need
To buy new teaching togs. Stand back! Disperse!
A pack of yokels round a raree show
Display more civilized restraint. What's this?

You say that Mary and her lamb have piqued you?
Would it were you had but half such zeal
For conning your assigned arithmetic!
How comes it, ask you, Mary's pet's so loyal—
Keeping watch all weathers, patiently,
With ne'er a reproving bleat nor grumbling baa?

The answer's simple, children. Have you marked
How cavalierly she ignores her pet,
Leaving him to languish by the gate?
Of course the lamb adores. Who could resist
Such fetching imperfection? It's the room
Improvement has for exercise that draws.
She spurns the lamb's devotion now, but wait:
Present grief's tomorrow's happiness.

Be lessoned, children: wise hearts want not ease
Nor seek success, but prize the balking thwart,
Find cheer in irksome checks, get gain from gall,
See good in bad. But scat! It's growing late.

I'm not paid overtime for this. Go home!
And mind you shut the door as you depart!

❧ THE DESERTED LAMB
Matthew Arnold

The sun lies soft upon the sward,
The drowsy air blows warm.
Across the flowered lawn a swarm
Of tireless bees, with random toil,
Improves the sultry hour;
And in the field, with labor hard,
The steady plower
Tills the heavy soil.

But, ah, how wan and wearisome
The busy hours become
When, through the drear and lonely days,
Languishes desire,
And hopes, deceived by long delays,
Sicken and expire.

Outside, alone, oh absent Mary,
Your lonely lamb repines.
My heart, by faithless love made wary,
Sees naught in Nature's vernal show
To brace my blighted soul—to grow
From my parched soil new vines.

Is love, then, a mirage, seen
In a wasted land of want?
Is constancy an empty vaunt
And faith an idle dream?
Are peace and joy and friendship, high endeavor and renown
But sound?

Ah, Mary, leave the straitening school,
The dim and dusky hall.
To fathom what dead sages meant
We forfeit calm and lose content.
He is a wrought and restless fool
Who answers Learning's siren call.

Alas, unheard, unheeded is my moan.
I live alone.
Like a mariner whom mutineers maroon
Upon a lush, uncharted isle,
Always, even in the night, while
Sleep delays its precious boon,
And ever in the brilliant day
He hears the murmurous hum of life,
Alien and near,
The noise of furred and feathered strife—
Grunts of lust, whimpers of fear,
Screams of things at bay.
But human accents never reach his ear—
Except his own unanswered prayer
Dying in the vacant air.

MISTRESS MARY
Dante Gabriel Rossetti

"O where are you going mystical maid,
       Mistress Mary?
You ascend the steps so serene and staid."
"I'm going to learn to write and read,
       Little lamb."
    (O Mary, Mistress Mary,
Going to school, twixt medieval and modern.)

"O why do you carry an offering so grand,
       Mistress Mary,
That blood red fruit within your hand?"
"It's a bribe no teacher can withstand,
       Little lamb."
    (O Mary, Mistress Mary,
Polishing apples, twixt medieval and modern.)

"In your hair is hyacinth and sweet pea,
       Mistress Mary,
And why do you carry a white lily?"
"I want the teacher to notice me,
       Little lamb."
    (O Mary, Mistress Mary,
Wearing posies, twixt medieval and modern.)

"On your girdle are broidered seven keys,
        Mistress Mary,
And rings arranged in symbolic threes."
"And in your fleece are several fleas,
        Little lamb."
    (O Mary, Mistress Mary,
Literal fleas, twixt medieval and modern.)

"Your eyelids droop with a heavy weight,
        Mistress Mary,
Your sighs are slumberous and opiate."
"I'm bored to tears with this tête-à-tête,
        Little lamb."
    (O Mary, Mistress Mary,
Going to sleep, twixt medieval and modern.)

"Who's that approaching figure, pray,
        Mistress Mary,
Robed in black and grizzled gray?"
"It's the teacher coming to send you away,
        Little lamb."
    (O Mary, Mistress Mary,
Good-bye little lamb, twixt medieval and modern.)

HYMN TO THE LAMB
Algernon Charles Swinburne

Oh barren and bookish and boring the insipid pursuit of Truth
That repays our passionate poring with profitless, impotent ruth,
And stuffy this stifling room, its scholars as stiff as dummies,
As a gloomy Egyptian tomb where Time tutors tractable
    mummies.
Oh flat and insipid the flavor of duty and discipline;
I seek the salt-sweet savor of permissive, insidious sin.
I thirst for the tangy-tart taste of iniquitous fruit forbidden;
I want to wallow and waste in Vice's voluptuous midden.
Simple sensations I spurn; all lawful delights I curse;
Kinky and quirky, I yearn for pleasures impure and perverse.
It's far-fetched and freakish frissons that attract, arouse and glut
The insatiable, glad-guilty greed of the sin-sated deviate.
With my peerlessly pliable pet, whose presence is poignantly
    missed,
I'll appease this feverish fret, as soon as school is dismissed.
With many a nip and a nibble, with debauched and abandoned
    biting,
We'll fidget and fritter and fribble and fondle in friendly-fierce
    fighting.
His insufferably sensuous fleece, his limbs, so lovely and lissome,
Will perturb, provoke and appease when I pummel, stroke and
    kiss 'em.
His eyes are lazy and lambent; his pelage, seductively sleek;
He's dreadfully dear when he's rampant, and cunningly cute when
    he's meek.

With kisses accursed we'll light a lurid, flaunting flame;
For others does love flicker bright; for us it shines on our shame.
We'll revel in ruinous riot, find bliss in baleful bane;
We'll stew in serene disquiet, pluck pleasure from piquing pain.
I suppose a sensible shrink might correct my craving for lambs,
But he couldn't cure me, I think, of scribbling dithyrambs.

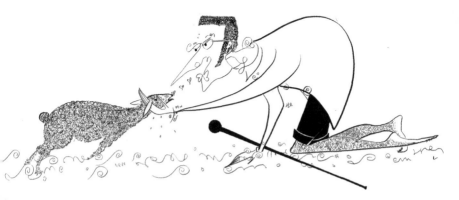

A SHROPSHIRE LAMB
A. E. Housman

I went to school, and I believe
That I could count past two
If the teacher had not made me leave
And filled my heart with rue.

Mary kissed me ere I left
And said I should not cry,
But now, heartbroken and bereft,
I've learned that lovers lie.

Now Mary's doing calculus
And trigonometry,
While I, alone and envious,
Have yet to get to three.

THE LAMBKIN: TO LADY MARY
Gerard Manley Hopkins

I got, just, a prize-piece of inreaching outsight,
Saw school-cloistered Mary's loyal lamb transgress,
Break bounds, fall mudpuddlewards—emerge a mickle-mottled
    muck-mess.
A piquant picture, a quaint quiddity? Quite!
Careless he frisks, sure that his Lady's bright
Absolving lavabo will tainted dirt-dress
Clean. But, ah! Disthoughting stress!
Can God-grace fail foul fleece: His boon-bath not wash white?

Perturbéd creature, peace! Here's, to proctor your gambols,
Mary. Lave! Fond salvific love scours span
Man, bird, beast and bug: grapples 'gainst ground-in grit and
    never trembles!
Never doubt! Wonders abound! Even poets can
Astound! Can turn plain facts to scintillant symbols,
Parse, plumb, and make sprung rhythm scan.

LAMBY
Rudyard Kipling

We marched right up to the school'ouse door, an' Mary she went in,
So I ups an' goes in after 'er, not meanin' any sin,
But 'arf way through I'm 'alted by a pukka muckamuck
Who sez, "I'll not 'ave beasts in 'ere," so I'm out o' school an' luck.
   O it's Lamby, look lively, an' Lamby, drop dead, an' Lamby, push
      and pull,
     But it's "Come right 'ere, you fuzzy dear" when it's time fer shearin'
       wool—
     When it's time fer shearin' wool, me mates, time fer shearin' wool,
     O it's "Come right 'ere, you fuzzy dear," when it's time fer shearin'
       wool.

The schoolmaster 'e drops names when 'e talks; I drops aitches and gees,
I ain't good enough fer 'im by 'arf; 'e calls me a beast, if yer please.
But I've won the 'eart of a plucky girl; the master 'e lives by 'isself
Readin' 'oity-toity 'ighbrow books lined up on 'is bloomin' shelf.
   O it's Lamby, speak out, an' Lamby, shut up, an' Lamby don't and do,
     But it's "Come right 'ere, you chubby dear," when it's time fer
      mutton stew—
     When it's time fer mutton stew, me mates, time fer mutton stew,
     O it's "Come right 'ere, you chubby dear," when it's time fer
      mutton stew.

AT SCHOOL
Thomas Hardy

At school a lamb leapt o'er the sill
And searched among the schoolgirls there,
Mary and Jenny and Polly and Gill
And lovely Lucy with curly hair,
Till Mary, conquering maidenly fear,
Embraced and kissed the wooly dear.

Though the master simulated ire
And gave the lamb a doorward shove,
Mary's act he did so admire
That he spoke to his class of reciprocal love.
The lamb overheard and, taking the cue,
Did not gainsay the dominie,
So innocent Mary never knew
'Twas Lucy the lamb went in to see.

LOCO LAMB AND THE SCHOOLMAN
William Butler Yeats

The schoolman threw me out the door,
My fleece was blacked with earth,
"No gamy lamb may learn," said he;
"You mar my day with mirth.
Consort with unruly, rancid ewes;
In a dunghill learn your worth."

"Order and odor are twins," I said,
"And ordure feeds the rose.
You don't smell so good yourself,
You wolf in scholar's clothes;
The bogus stench of sanctity
Offends my brutish nose.

"Don't teach my Mary argument,
Who is by grace made wise.
Be schooled by your pupil, pedagogue,
Before you moralize;
No magus mounts until he kneels
In the sty where Godhead lies."

LAMB

D. H. Lawrence

Outside the window in the deep, dark shadow of the huge,
    brooding, root-deep, life-asserting oak tree,
Mary saw her lamb
Gleaming,
Its soft, suave, electric fleece
Richly gleaming,
White, secret-white, and subtle,
In the awful, blind, quick-deep darkness of the sap-rapt, silent oak.

And she was frightened,
Exposed and frightened.

The unutterable mystery of the lone, aloof lamb,
Obscurely gleaming,
Penetrated her.
To the very plasma of her plexus she was penetrated,
And a deep, obscure spasm of dark blood-knowledge stirred in her
    womb,
And she was exposed,
Unutterably exposed,
Open to the stark, male assertion of the lamb.

Half she hated it,
This blind, effaced lamb-force.
Half she wanted it,
This impersonal, blood-deep submission to the blind, naked
    lamb-force.

Inside the schoolroom the sardonic, bird-like master prated of love
And exulted,
Wickedly exulted,
That the lamb was now expelled.

Phaugh! How she hated this talk of love!
The master moved his small beak-mouth and chattered, as
    jackdaws do,
Moved his mouth, making abhorrent, mocking sounds, as
    chattering jackdaws do.

He *would* chatter, with his slack, pallid face and hideous, lapsed eyes,
Would force her with his heavy, heavy will,
Would preach and prate with his nervous, sinister neurasthenic
    voice,
Would, demon-like, force her mercilessly into the soul-tearing
    anguish of intimate, personal love.

Nay!
Away, black hell-bird!
Volare!
Her soul refused his fatal, willful knowledge.

She averted her gaze from the brittle finality of the false ego-bound
    master
And looked outside
And dreamed of mindless, dark submission to the lamb
In the deep, dark darkness.

❧ LITTLE GAFFER
T. S. Eliot

I am old, I am old,
My feet are cold.
In an empty schoolroom memories prick
The cicatrix of past desire;
Ghostly fingers probe the tender quick
Of dead regret.
I am alone.

That distant springtime when we met,
Mary, the lamb girl, embraced her pet,
Her golden hair stirred by favonian breezes,
Her arms full of lanose flocculence.
I am racked by grippes, catarrhs, and wheezes;
I wear long flannel underpants.

While others found the living truth,
I spoke of love to callow youth.

I never sailed with Shaftoe's crew,
Neither, at Banbury Cross, saw the ringéd dame ride by,
Nor stuck my thumb in pie.
Never, on the fatal count of two,
Dared to buckle my shoe.

When do old thoughts come to rest?
Do they live in pluperfect eternity,
Or die in the future when the present is past,
Or in the present when the future has not come to pass,
Or directly after tea?

An old man.
Mold and memory.
Baa baa baa.

❧ A REFUSAL TO BLEAT AND MOAN
ABOUT BEING EXPELLED FROM SCHOOL
Dylan Thomas

Un-Edened in lapsed wormriddled spring,
Bounced and virgin shorn,
Of mankind's mind-made letters fleeced
And brothered by maculate sex-spawned things,
I shall not mourn
The broken plights of fallen flesh.

Short shriven in time's green fevered toil
By a loin-dry don,
I will not mar with inconsonant pleas
The dumb wind's pregnant phrase nor spoil
The fluent din
Of analphabetic jays and bees.

Applewise in the fell beatitudes of bud
And spasm-spewn seed,
Murdering world dam, be my Mary;
Gravely conduct the holy hubbub
Of strain and breed,
Retort with stuff to man's daft query.

It's cocktail hour at a chic urban bar. Springtime. Mary, an habitué, is engaging in trivial banter with a prepossessing young fellow who claims to be "in finance." Mary, in her thirty-seventh year, has something of a reputation. To her ill-suppressed irritation, at class reunions she is invariably remembered as a lamb-loving innocent. But over the years, among her more urbane city friends and associates, she has attained to a different kind of dubious eminence: she has acquired what people refer to as "a name for herself." Mary urgently wants the child she never had and a husband—one utterly different from the handsome bastard she married and from whom she had been divorced for . . . how long now? Twelve years! Suppressing a stab of stark panic, Mary smiles and orders another Mai Tai.

Mary thinks—
I was taught wrong. That's my trouble.
Taught to be trusting. Taught to think
Love, given, leads to love
Reciprocated. Silly cant!
I've had to learn that lovers and lambs
Are quite different quantities.
But I can't lay it all on bad education.
That would be neat, but not really true.
I knew, or at least I quickly learned,
Men are louts, and yet I liked 'em.
What can you do? Wishes aren't choices.
Choices are given, by chance, it seems,
And either you pick from what options there are
Or you don't play at all, and solitaire
Becomes your game, safe but insipid.
What's more, it's spring—pushy spring,
Promoting its prime imperatives.
Jonquil and pansy, just promoted,

Laugh at restraint, and playing the lenient
Seneschals of creation's estate,
Commend the breaking of bounds before
You're checked by Death's stiff discipline.
Oh, the hapless heart's a giddy guide
Through the parlous passes of passionate love—
A risky bet, a weak reed,
A feckless hound that follows you home.

Mary says—
"What did you say your name was? Norman?
Well, Norm, whaddaya say?
It's been a gas, gabbin' like this.
Now, what's your pleasure? Your place or mine?"

SCHOOL GOING
Philip Larkin

It's vacant now, the sightless windows shattered.
A null, numbing wind's the only sound
Where, a life ago, children chattered—
Champing, school-chafed colts, keen to bound
Outdoors, to escape the fusty, wordy fart
Maundering on as though his lessons mattered.
Weather's work and the tick of time will do in
The best devices of the builder's art.
The school still stands, but now, like me, a ruin.

There's talk of sprucing up this seedy relic,
Placing a plaque, playing the tourist game:
"This is the site of that renowned bucolic . . ."
Bilge! Who cares? What a shoddy claim
To worth that once a pupil brought a lamb
To school and that I gave its rump a kick.
Forget this rank rat manor! Let it rot,
Along with all those antiquated, sham
Homilies on loyal love I taught.

Mary (she never did) is now deceased.
She slept around and didn't give a damn
For consequences till the good times ceased
And syphilis took her off. As for the lamb,
Mary's father did not share his daughter's
Sentimental fondness for the beast,
Whose place, he knew, would soon be filled by chaps.
A realistic bloke, he had it slaughtered
And sliced its carcass up for roasts and chops.

And me? Decrepitude has not yet shut
Me altogether down. Toothless, I dribble
The insipid pap I'm fed down tie and shirt,
But still I live. At least I don't spout drivel
About pure lovey-lamby agape.
I dread death. I have no recourse but
To hug the refuse of the thieving years:
Tapioca with café au lait.
A lovely lie-down after lunch. Tears.

❦ SECOND THOUGHTS ABOUT MARY
Stevie Smith

After Mary's lamb's brusque rout,
The children, struck by its loyalty,
Asked their teacher why it hung about
And got an improving homily
To the general effect that if one loves another,
The other, perforce, loves the lover.

But I must rebut with a blunt demurral:
The facts don't support the moral.

For Mary did not love the lamb.
She was old enough for school—at least six—
A standard, stock schoolgirl, sick
Of puerile romps with her lamb.

I think Mary loved Billy McSwigan.
I think that she had already developed an eye
For his roguish grin
And his boyish swank.

Mary was embarrassed by the lamb.
She was, in fact, trying to ditch him.
The teacher had twigged to her
And knew perfectly well that his lesson was lame.

In short, the teacher fabled.
Oh, no doubt, not to lie *per se*;
To protect innocence, he might well say
That bending truth is merely a foible.

And it is a pretty story, is it not,
His tale of autogenous devotion,
Of predictable, pat reciprocation?
I love; therefore, you love.
Tit for tat.

Yes, it is pretty.
I like it too.
But it is not adult, not true.
Mary was bored with tame, innocent larks,
She found them flat and petty.
She had already guessed what idylls lack:
Reality and risk.
Mary was ready for sex.

Oh yes, I know, you are shocked.
Even at this late post-Freudian hour we are shocked.
We try to be shockless and chic;
We try to think it's remote and antique—
That noisy ruction over infant sexuality,
But our reactions won't pass modern muster:
At heart we sympathize with Mary's master.
We want to believe in purity.

But when we do not get what we wanted,
We must learn not to lie about what's gotten,
We must be honest and disenchanted.
Mendacity, not Mary's rotten.

I dedicate this book to all thirty-two of the English poets whose styles I have adopted and to one other poet—though I can't say for certain who he or she is. I'm referring to the author of "Mary Had a Little Lamb." Because the authorship of this nursery rhyme is often attributed to Mother Goose, I've gone along with tradition. In fact, there are two compelling reasons for believing that Mother Goose is not the author. First, the poem originally appeared in print as the work of the American poet Sarah Josepha Hale, and, second, Mother Goose does not exist. But there is also a fairly convincing reason for contending that Hale may not have been the sole author of the poem. If oral tradition is to be believed, she appropriated and added to a four-stanza poem written by John Roulstone. This poem—the one reproduced in this book—is the one that has achieved worldwide fame. Alas, there is no hard documentary evidence that Roulstone wrote it, and Hale always adamantly insisted that his claim to authorship was a fraud. What's certain is that some actual, living person wrote "Mary Had a Little Lamb" and that I have further obscured that person's claim to fame by knowingly and deliberately ascribing authorship of the poem to a fiction. I am sorry for that, but perhaps this explanatory note will to some slight degree serve to illuminate my dilemma and mitigate my guilt.

ACKNOWLEDGMENTS

Many people have been instrumental in the gathering of my otherwise wayward lambs into a single, coherent volume. First and foremost, heartfelt thanks to Sue Berger Ramin, shepherdess extraordinaire, who discovered them and gave them a home at Brandeis University Press. Thanks also to Kate Feiffer who found them, words on a page, and brought them to vibrant life. And to Lisa Diercks who designed for them the deluxe accommodations that they now inhabit. I am boundlessly grateful to these wonderful ladies and, indeed, to all of the people at Brandeis University Press who have been unfailingly kind and obliging. For permission to republish, I also wish to express my appreciation of Dr. John Lamb, editor of *Victorian Poetry*, the journal in which my first parodies originally appeared. And for her staunch support and invaluable assistance, special thanks and loving gratitude to my wife, Roberta.

ABOUT THE AUTHOR AND ILLUSTRATOR

David R. Ewbank is professor emeritus of English Literature at Kent State University. He has authored *Fairy Tales for Adults* and *A Distant Summer*, and he served as co-editor of the multivolume collection *The Complete Works of Robert Browning*. He lives in Ohio.

Kate Feiffer's illustrations have appeared in magazines, newspapers, and on television. She is the author of eleven highly acclaimed children's books, including *Henry the Dog with No Tail* and *My Mom is Trying to Ruin My Life*, and the event producer for the Martha's Vineyard–based writers festival Islanders Write. She lives on Martha's Vineyard and in New York.